# A Book
# of
# Accidental Cats

## Hilary Orme

ISBN: 9798693240537

# Contents

# ACKNOWLEDGMENTS

Rebecca Jackson for the use of her artwork,
*The Fearless Five.*
All other images were created from the author's own
photographs using *Lunapic* software.

# ABOUT

'There are no ordinary cats,' Colette, the French writer once wrote. This collection of poems celebrates the extraordinary cats that I have met across the years. Some have seized large slices of my life in their tenacious claws, while others have padded softly on the fringes of my existence.

Some have drawn blood, or presented me with a dead mouse at three in the morning, while others have existed only in those ephemeral, virtual worlds, such as Twitter.

It matters little where I have encountered them, because each one has left an indelible paw mark on my being. They have brought joy and sadness in equal measure; they have engendered a sense of awe and wonder, frustration and pleasure and in times of trouble, they have brought solace, soothing unease with their healing purrs. Sadly, they have also visited me with grief at their loss.

Now, I invite you to meet my clowder and to share their stories.

# The Cat Who Walks

You may ask where I am going,
But I will never tell
Of my secret, well-worn pathways
In forest and in dell.

You will never see my valley,
A misty bowl of milk,
Or a newly-birthed conker
On a bed of silk.

You will not find my hedgerows,
Berry, bauble-bright,
Or hear the soft wind singing
In the treetops late at night.

The prayer-book musty mushrooms
Where the belladonnas sleep
Entangled in the Old Man's Beard,
Are secrets I will keep.

You will not hear the migrant birds
That chatter on the wire,
Or hunt in piles of leaf leather,
The summer's funeral pyre.

You will not feel the icy blast
Shake slumbering poppy seeds
From ripe and wizzened pepper pots,
And hide them in the weeds.

You may ask where I am going,
But I will never tell
Of my secret, well-worn pathways
In forest and in dell.

# Hunter's Moon

With body low and ears held high,
My nose and whiskers to the sky,
I glide on velvet paws, unseen
On orchard paths and in between
Trees hung with apple, plum and pear.
I pause, I poise and taste the air.
A shadow in the shade I slide,
From trees to field at hedgerow side.
'Neath beech and holly and hawthorn,
I pass into the stubble-corn.
Softly, softly,  paddle-paws,
Crouching low on all fours,
I am set to spring, ambush, attack,
When from the night a phantom, black,
Scoops me up and takes me home,
Safe inside no more to roam.
On my rug I knead and purr
While firelight glistens on my fur,
But in my dream, way up high,
A Hunter's Moon hangs in the sky.

# Anythingarian

Cinnamon-coated, glitter-glazed,
The Bengal lopes, leopard-like
Through undergrowth, head raised,
Steel of eye and flint of claw.

Marshmallow melt, placid puff-ball,
The Ragdoll slides softly down,
And gazes up with eyes that call
To the deep sea blue and the sky above.

Round of head, and eye and paw
The British Shorthair smiles and all
Around him sing his praises and adore
His comfortable, fireside face.

You, my friend are all of these, complete:
A mix of every sweet-natured breed in part,
As you wind yourself around my feet
And purr love into my heart.

# Yoga for Cats

The transcendental tabby slid into the room.
She rolled her mat across the floor,
Faced her class with commanding grace,
And lifted an elegant paw.

Sweet, purring music drifted round,
All pupils took up their poses:
The Cat, The Child or the Downward Dog,
Tails higher than their noses.

They started with a Tabletop, facing to the ground,
Then stretched and arched a Camel Back,
Adopting next the Warrior Two,
Before pausing for a snack.

The transcendental tabby slid out of the room,
But waited at the door to peek
At twenty sleeping cats, curled up -
The same happens every week.

# All Hallows' Eve

She lived alone on top of a hill
Beneath a sky so dark and vast,
That its billion stars told the world's long tale
Of present, future, past.

The Plough, the Bull and Orion's Belt,
To the firmament did cleave,
As she craned to see the zenith point
On that All Hallows' Eve.

The moon rose slowly in the east
And touched everything in sight:
The brook became a silver stream,
The fields were stardust bright.

Tinselled branches, finger-like,
Snatched at  bats that trawl
The cold still air, that echoed to
The barn owl's mournful call.

Late cabbages, silent sentries stood
Guard at the parsnip bed,
Lace-edged against the crystal grass
And the white-roofed garden shed.

Once safe inside, the door was locked;
For a moment, she lingered still
And watched the magic of the night
From her kitchen window sill.

The washing line, a diamond necklace danced,
In a gentle, whispering breeze
And an eerie, other-worldly sound
Murmured through the trees.

"Moonstruck," she cried, as she turned and saw
A spectre, pooled by light,
It's eyes sparked like the stars above,
A puff-ball, moonlight-bright.

"Are you friendly, phantom?" she asked the cat.
The cat gave no reply,
But tilted its head and tipped its chin
And slowly closed its eye.

When autumn comes and the fires are lit
In that cottage late at night,
Luna stays inside on All Hallows' Eve
And bathes in the cool moonlight

Though the doors are locked and the curtains drawn,
A moonbeam creeps through a breach
And for a moment, her blues eyes spark,
Then she curls up out of reach.

She turns three times on the open lap,
Settles, paw over her nose,
And dreams of galaxies' worlds afar
That only Luna knows.

She listens to the moonbeam's call
To wander once again,
But a gentle hand smooths down her fur:
It's here she will remain.

# My Name

I am a cat of a thousand names, and I answer not to one.
In ancient times, you called me *Bast*, the daughter of the sun.
You worshipped and adored me then, in fertility and war;
The gift of life and serenity, lay underneath my paw.

I am a cat of a thousand names, and I answer not to one.
As *Bygul* and *Trjegul*, Freya's chariot I would run.
I would ride with the Valkyries and chose who would be slain,
Then lead them to Valhalla, where they would live again.

I am a cat of a thousand names, and I answer not to one.
To Newton, I was *Spithead*, and when his work was done,
He made a cat flap for my young, so that they'd not make a fuss,
But follow me in silence and not disturb his Calculus.

I am a cat of a thousand names, and I answer not to one.
With *Grimalkin* as the witch's cat, Macbeth was soon undone.
The sky above was ruptured with the  Weird Sisters' cries,
And all men came to learn, my dark name to despise.


I am a cat of a thousand names and I answer not to one.
So when you call me late at night, your summons I will shun,
For I have answered every alias, and not one will I own,
For each cat has its secret name… and it is never  known.

# Cat o'Clock

At two in the morning, I open one eye,
Settle my haunches and, with a sigh
Hear the wind roaring and pounding rain
Lashing against the window pane.

By three o'clock, it's calm and still,
So I start to wail, so loud and shrill
That my human servant leaps out of bed,
Rubs her eyes and holds her head.

She shuffles and stumbles towards the door,
Opens it wide, waits, then implores,
"Are you going out?" as I sniff night airs,
Then turn and run back up the stairs.

Wearily, she leaves a window wide,
So that I can choose when to go outside.
By four o'clock I have caught a mouse
And brought my gift into the house.

At five, I thought the mouse was dead,
Until it scuttled off under the servant's bed.
Although I have tried again and again,
Humans are impossible to train!

At six, her hunting skills still scant,
She replaces them with a ferocious rant.
Using words I do not wish to know,
She finally traps it and *lets it go!*

Bleary-eyed, at seven, I see her crawl
To the kitchen, where I start to bawl;
I turn and pace around her feet,
Until with breakfast, I'm replete.

She leaves for work, just after eight,
But only gets to the garden gate:
Fuzzy-headed and weary, she forgot
Her car keys. She has lost the plot!

Alone at nine, I'm tired and fed,
So I take myself to the servant's bed,
Where I make a nest on her pure white sheet
And dream of fish and cream and meat.

# The Ballad of Alice the Book Store Cat

Alice was a book store cat, who lived on velvet green.
In a wonderland of words she reigned,
The undisputed queen.

By day, she slept on dusty shelves 'tween 'Diplomacy' and 'Care',
Or sometimes in 'Good Manners',
For few disturbed her there.

At five o'clock, Old Marchen drew the blinds against the night,
Then sat and read aloud to her
By gentle firelight.

And in each tale, she'd see herself, the Queen of Derring Do:
She'd sit astride a unicorn,
Or sail the ocean blue.

The back room was a shrine to poetry and prose,
Where each word conjured up the worlds
That only Alice knows.

At midnight on a winter's eve, when all was calm and still,
She'd slip outside into the Square,
And sing a song so shrill,

That all the cats from miles around would gather at her feet,
And listen there, in wonder
To her stories so complete

That they would marvel at her tales of myst'ry and romance
And paw in paw upon the green,
'Til first light they would dance.

Now if by chance you pass that way, upon a winter's night,
Do not disturb their carousel,
It is the rarest sight.

In memory of Alice the Book Store Cat, who was adopted by the
Dusty Bookshelf, Lawrence, Kansas in 1997 and lived there until
her death in 2014.

# The Cat in the Window

On Christmas Eve, the clowder met,
Grey and cold, weak and wet.
It watched the shoppers rushing past,
Speeding homeward, free at last.

Six eyes of amber, gold and green,
Lit up the alley's dismal scene
And fixed with an unwavering gaze,
The pet shop, just across the way.

The church bell signalled closing time,
But each was heedless of its chime.
Instead, they watched a kitten stare
From the window, lone and bare.

Mu, with green-glass eyes stood up:
He used to sup from  gilded cup
Until the colour-scheme was changed
And his departure was arranged.

Luna, sweet as moonbeams, light and fair
Drifted down on the soft night air.
Here, her kittens came in a wheelie bin,
And there they faded, weak and thin.

Captain Jack - three legs, one eye, one ear,
Shivered, not with cold but instead with fear,
For once he had been complete and whole,
Until torment and cruelty took their toll.

Suddenly, six eyes flashed bright,
As a child appeared in the fading light,
And pressed his nose to the window pane,
And cried 'I want!', again and again.

His care-worn mother came to see
What had filled her son with glee,
But a chill wind from the alley way
Made her drag her child away.

A lady passed the window black,
Stopped, smiled and then turned back,
And to the kitten sadly said,
'You're so like my Captain Fred.'

The shop bell rang, she went inside:
Carrying a box with care and pride,
She stepped onto the path again,
But something made her cross the lane.

There she held the box on high,
And with a heartfelt, passionate cry
Made a pledge to the empty night,
To let them know it would be all right.

"This cat is not a plaything,
This  cat is not a toy.
I will give this cat her dignity
And she will bring me joy!"

A gust of wind, and bright lights flashed,
A  touch of warmth rushing past,
And in the starlit sky she heard
A gentle sound, as three cats purred.

# The Rescuer

As snow fell down on fallen snow,
The deep earth frozen, far below,
The savage squalls raged without rest
And sculpted snow, a chiselled crest.

A mother, with her offspring small,
Found refuge near a fallen wall.
Sparse shelter for her newborn young,
That clustered close and to her clung.

Five lives were ebbing fast away,
When through the blizzard at close of day,
A solitary man came at last,
Head bent against the stinging blast.

He took them home with gentle haste,
A warm heart in that icy waste.
For those who love the smallest, find
They are the greatest of mankind.


This poem is dedicated to Hans Halden, in recognition of all the work he does with Forente Poter (United Paws), an organisation that rescues cats in Norway.

# Cat on a Greek Island

Rendered white, the sun-bleached walls
Beat back the mid-day sun,
And heat-cupped courtyards
Simmered in the open glare.
In the quiet square, a feral cat furled
Before the door of Saint Sebastian.
Behind its half-sealed eyes,
Flickered dreams of cool alleyways,
Where food and fights and
Friendship were easy prey.

# Inspector Paw of the Yard

Inspector Paw of the Yard follows every trail:
He finds his quarry every time. He's never known to fail.
Nose to the ground in hot pursuit, he rarely will be seen,
As he slides down streets and avenues, and slips in between
Trees on wide boulevards, and like a shadow glides,
But no-one knows  where he lurks, or behind which bush he hides.

He examines all the clues with great scrutiny and care:
He tips his nose up to the sky and gently tastes the air.
No-one knows the boundaries of his immeasurable patrol.
His beat is every dustbin, each cupboard and mouse hole.
He checks cat flap security, when he's working underground
And cleans the kitchen dishes, in case rodents are around.

He was a tale told to kittens, when they would not go to bed,
'Inspector Paw will come for you!' is what the grown ups said.
They would scurry to their baskets, and with paws over their eyes,
Would tremble as they saw him pass, a master of disguise.
Inspector Paw of the Yard follows every trail:
He finds his quarry every time. He's never known to fail.

# Arthur the Aga Cat

Arthur the Aga Cat sleeps, sly-eyed against the simmering plate,
While in his dreams, he drifts between barn and stall,
His quarry-quest complete, he returns, mouth laden with prey,
Limp and lifeless, and lays his offering in the hall.

As he nestles on the oven, he sees the household passing by;
Sometimes behind the wainscot, an unwary mouse will stir,
But his eyelids barely flicker and you'll see no more
Than a single whisker's twitch, or hear a little lion's purr.

He replays his age of prowess, when in those younger days,
With fire in his belly, he'd prowl and rage and roar.
He was Lord of the Yard and King of the Hill,
Ruling his domain with growling power and iron paw.

For a moment, Arthur stretches, toes splayed and back arched,
Then, curled like a comma round the hot plate cover,
Returns again to his toasted fantasies  and yearns to be
A fearsome, fiery fighter and a riggish, red hot lover.

# The Indifference of Cats

My friend the dog yaps and barks
And wears his heart on his paw;
While I disdain and turn my back
And leave you wanting more.

You bribe me with expensive gifts,
which I sniff and then ignore,
I prefer to chase a piece of string
Around the kitchen floor.

My bed, a thing of beauty is,
Of tweed and fur, so fine,
But at 3 a.m. I claim *your* bed -
Which of course, by rights is mine.

The dog adores and worships you
With eyes that sadly shine,
But I enslave you with one look
By slowly blinking mine.

# My Favourite Curtains ( or why they now have blinds)

When I was a kitten,
I'd climb to the top,
Then someone would hold me,
And scold me,
And tell me to stop.

When I was a young cat
Behind them I'd hide,
But they would find me,
And remind me,
That cats go outside.

When I was an adult,
Loose threads I would claw,
But they would chide me,
And deride me,
And tap me on the paw.

Now I am an old cat,
Those curtains I shred,
They've bequeathed me,
And beneath me
Are now part of my bed.

# Cat Conundrum

To you it is a mystery, an enigma and a puzzle,
When I turn three times upon the mat, then race off at the
double.
You are often in a quandary when you see me on the roof,
Surveying all my kingdom, remote and so aloof.

Although I have a basket, in which to lay my head,
I lie down on the laptop or in the middle of your bed.
The bowl of clean water that you put down every day,
I leave and search out puddles, to your horror and dismay.

To you I am a paradox, a giant question mark:
When you are ready for your bed, I'm hunting in the dark.
I am a great conundrum, a problem to be solved.
How can I watch an empty wall and seem so much involved?

To you, it is a riddle when I stretch out on my back,
Then as you stroke my belly, I launch a wild attack.
For one thing that is certain, no matter how you look,
Each cat to every human is a secret and closed book.

# Four of my Nine

I was the giant's child,
But to him I was so small,
He barely noticed me at all.

I was the ogre's child,
But sometimes I would catch his eye
And know he saw me in a pie.

I was the witch's child,
But eye of newt and toe of frog
Were nothing more than wash of hog.

So I became the woman's child.

She lays her tributes at my feet,
Calls me 'Precious' , 'Diddums' ,'Sweet'.
She lets me lie upon her bed,
Chucks my chin and strokes my head.
But there is one thing I decline:
She thinks I'm *hers*, but she is *mine*.

# The Music of the Night

Hollow dog barks ring the farmyard wall,
The high wood echoes to the barn owl's call.
A blunt-nosed mole, without a sound
Softly turns sodden earth beneath the ground.

Along his watchtower the tom cat crawls,
Stepping softly on ivied walls.
From a ragged branch a late leaf flutters,
Then along the path, limps and stutters.

A siren scream pierces the still night air,
The vixen lures her dog fox from his lair.
Cock pheasants in their roosts close by,
Take up the alarm and soar to the sky.

# After Passchendaele

As a student working late,
I'd pass out by the southern gate.
My homeward path along a track,
Passed tidy terraces, back-to-back.
At one I'd stop beneath a tree,
Where a brindled tabby greeted me.
She rubbed against my legs and purred,
But ears and whiskers suddenly stirred
As she heard a haunting sound;
A sobbing, yelling, rang around
That peaceful part of Worcestershire,
Far from war, far from fear.
He'd rant and rave and then he'd cry,
"Why did they not let *me* die?"
Then raging, to his wife he'd call,
"Why did *I* alone not fall?"
For he had fought at Passchendaele,
And he had lived to tell the tale
Of where many of his comrades fell
In that blood-soaked, quagmire hell.

Now as I lean upon my fork
And watch my tabby slowly walk
On good, dark earth between the rows
Of cabbages and potatoes,
I stand and dwell on his sacrifice,
The lives we lost at such a price.
The debt that every person owes,
For it is in peace, that prosperity grows.

## The Fearless Five

I am the Salty Sea Cat, and sail I the ocean wide,
On the Good Ship Fiona, my crew right by my side.
With Billy O, Bob and Megan and Grandma  (galley slave),
I scan the horizon for the sailors I will save.


We have sailed in choppy waters, been stranded on a rock,
Thwarted thieves and kidnappers, and caused visitors to flock
To see me swim in the harbour, then round the docks I rove,
Seeking out ham sandwiches and hidden treasure trove.


I dream of my adventures and, whenever she is near,
I give stories to my servant, which  I whisper in her ear.
I go over every detail, so that she will not forget,
But leave aside the secret that my feet never get wet.

The Salty Sea Cat's adventures are chronicled in the children's books, *Past the Town of Tribulation and Straight on to Derring Do, Red Skye Sunset, The Intrepid Trotter Malloy* and *Pevensey the Pirate King.*

*Illustration by Rebecca Jackson*

# The Office Cat
(Or Why My Work Did Not Get Finished)

The cat is on the keyboard,
The cat is on the chair,
The cat is on the bookshelf,
That cat is everywhere

Her paws are on the printer,
Her paws are on the screen
Her paws are ripping paper
From the copying machine.

Her tail's across the notepad,
Her tail's across the keys,
Her tail is knocking pens off
With the greatest of ease.

# Hollow

There is a hollow on the bed
Where you would sleep at night,
So soft and warm and gentle,
You stayed 'til morning light.

Now there's a hollow by the tree,
Where you would play and roam.
I laid you there in sodden earth.
Now, you're forever home.

Now there's a hollow in my heart
That nothing seems to fill.
I cannot hold you anymore,
But you are with me still.

There is a hollow on the bed,
Small and soft and round,
Where you would sleep on winter nights
When frost was on the ground.


In memory of my cat, Dibbley, who was a
mighty panfur.

# Paw Notes on the Poems

*The Cat Who Walks* was inspired by the beautiful countryside in which I live. I have used snatches of this poem in many of my stories. Most notably, the words echo the opening paragraphs of *Sacrifice*, in *Twisted Tales: A Collection of Short Stories*.

'My spirits always rise with the hill. As I crest the brow, I am constantly surprised by the beauty of this place. In winter, the knoll wears a diadem of white crystal, barbed, ebony black against the leaden sky. In springtime, the summit is crowned with clouds of May blossom, while in summer, waves of soft, green grass flow to the valley below, rippling in the upland breeze. But the hill is never as beautiful as it is in autumn. The ridge, a gold-edged saucer brims with milk-warm mists; the hedgerows stand bauble-bright with haws, hips, sloes and blackberries and the lane is laid with a carpet of leaf-leather. From the silken lining of a spiked horse chestnut shell, a glossy conker is birthed. Thorns on a bed of silk: a reminder of the contrasts of a season caught between summer and winter, between life and death.

The prayer book mustiness of mushrooms and wood fires fills the air. A prayer of remembrance for lost seasons, written on the rustling pages of fallen leaves. Apple-rosy men, working in the fields, turn their collars against the chilly air, which foretell the icy blasts that will soon cut adrift the last lingering leaves and shake the slumbering poppy seeds from their pepper pots. Migrant birds chatter on the wire, exchanging travellers' tales before taking flight.

And I, a wanderer, return time and time again.'

*Hunter's Moon* was inspired by my cat's nocturnal activities. In the autumn, she is reluctant to observe the cat curfew, and often has to be encouraged to return home. One night, I was working late in the office, which overlooks the garden and the orchard beyond, when I caught a glimpse of her stalking her prey. The full moon is a cat's favourite hunting time, when it can fully utilise its night vision to outmanoeuvre unwary prey.

'Winterfylleth' was the name given to the month of October by the Anglo-Saxons. The words for 'winter' and 'full moon' were combined to mark the beginning of the season, which followed the last full moon of the month. The moon has played an important part in many cultures. Here is a list of the names given to the moon at different times of the year, by the Algonquin tribes of Lake Superior.

January: Wolf Moon
February: Snow Moon
March (start): Worm Moon
March (end): Sap Moon
April: Pink Moon
May: Flower Moon
June: Strawberry Moon
July: Buck Moon
August: Sturgeon Moon
September: Harvest Moon
October: Hunter's Moon
November: Beaver Moon
December: Cold Moon

In my children's series about the *Salty Sea Cat*, I make several references to the moon, and its importance to sailors, as Megan learns in Red Skye Sunset:

'Billy O had told me the difference between spring tides and neap tides. I knew that spring tides had nothing to do with the season, but that they happen when the sun and the moon line up, usually around the times of the new moon and the full moon. This means the sun and moon can work together to pull the waters of the Earth more strongly and this causes the water to rise higher. On the other hand, neap tides happen when the moon is waxing or waning and is at right angles to the sun. That means that they are pulling in different directions and the result is smaller tides.'

*Anythingarian* is my tribute to all of the cats that have ever owned me. Most have been rescue cats, sometimes adopted singly and sometimes in pairs. I have never lived with more than two cats at any time, although the temptation to do so, has been great. Aunt Caro, in *Born A Crow*, one of the short stories from *Twisted Tales*, would not have approved.

'Aunt Caro was famous for her outspokenness. She issued proclamations such as, 'Anyone with more than two cats is eccentric' or, 'A man with a collection of hats is certifiable, especially when that collection contains a pith helmet!'
Aunt Caro possessed only one cat and one hat. The cat, Max, was a puffball of Persian Blue. He was part child, part confidante. Every evening, she would place him on her lap and groom his long, tangled fur. As she did so, they would discuss both important and trivial matters, cheek by jowl. She made little distinction between the Suez Crisis and the collision of the *Home and Colonial* boy's bicycle with her hollyhocks.
Her single hat was revered as much as Max. It was a pheasant. Not a whole pheasant, of course, but a cock pheasant's most iridescent plumage, wrapped creatively around a black felt crown. From the awe and wonder level of a ten year old, it appeared that a bird was quietly nesting amongst Aunt Caro's fine, silvery hair. I was always unsure which I held in the highest regard, Max or The Hat.'

*Yoga for Cats* was inspired by Gladstone, one of the Cabinet Cats. He lives and works as a mouser at H. M. Treasury and has over seventy-thousand followers on Twitter. Each Wednesday evening, he runs his online yoga class, where cats are encouraged to engage in poses that would prove difficult for humans, but are first nature to felines. Twitter has a large cat community, which generally promotes kindness and care, alongside a great deal of good humour. Gladstone has a number of 'Ambassacats' who share details of lost cats, useful advice and other forms of mutual support. Humans could learn a lot from the Cats of Twitter.

*All Hallows' Eve* is based on a short story, which was taken from one of my Blog posts. In Victorian times, Christmas Eve was the time to share ghost stories around the fireside, and I, wishing to uphold the tradition, shared this one in 2017.

'The light of the Full Cold Moon filled her kitchen. It had turned the running tap into a silver stream and dusted the work tops with a luminescent glow. Through the window, the early frost had transformed the garden into a fantastic landscape: white-coated branches, like spiky fingers snatched at Will o' the Wisp grasses that danced tantalisingly beneath them. The washing line had become a diamond necklace, and delicate, lace-edged cabbages, like silent sentries, stood guard over the vegetable patch. The moonlight was so bright that she had not needed to switch on the kitchen light, and now stood washing her supper dishes in the half-light, enchanted by its ethereal beauty.

The memory of a paper moon that had hung above her seventy years before, crept into her mind. She had been proud to be chosen to play *Yum-Yum* in her school's production of *The Mikado*, and still remembered every word of her songs. She hummed quietly as she washed her cup and placed it on the draining board. By the time she had reached the knives and forks, the sound had grown, until finally, the words had burst out of her, and she turned her face upwards to address the moon directly,

*"Ah pray make no mistake, we are not shy*
*We're very wide awake, the Moon and I"*

It was what she did - sing songs, that is. Her voice had become slightly more breathy with age, and it sometimes cracked on the high notes, but singing still gave her immense pleasure. After all, there was no-one to please but herself. Every room of the house had its own collection of songs, each linked to a person or a memory. As she walked up the stairs at night, she would be one step behind her husband as, shoulder high, he had carried the children to bed. 'The Grand Old Duke of York' had always extended their journey from the foot of the staircase to the top step. He had marched up and down in time to the rhyme, as the children had giggled and begged for more. She would sometimes repeat the actions as she went to bed now, pausing half way up to smile at the photograph of her son and daughter on the wall. They had been caught in time: her son a chubby-cheeked school boy in short trousers and next to him, her daughter looking like a puppet master who was very much in control. She had always pulled the strings, that one. In the end, she had pulled them so hard that she had whisked her son-in-law and grandchildren across the sea, all the way to Canada, where they had lived for the past forty years. Dutifully, her daughter rang once a week, although of late it had slipped to once a fortnight. At least it was something. Her son was less than fifty miles away, but her contact with him had diminished to a card at Christmas, and occasionally one on her birthday. He made the excuse that he was no good at letter writing, or that his phone had no credit. Two years ago, he had surprised her with a visit, but she had been relieved when, after an hour of small talk, he had made his excuses and left. Memories were the best company. She had carefully wrapped and preserved them in her songs, like her aunt's best china in the attic. Each night when the Grand Old Duke's journey was done, the tempo would change as she passed the empty nursery. There her voice would soften and *Brahms Lullaby* would carry her to her bedroom. As she got ready for bed, she would sing, *Beautiful Dreamer*. It had been her husband's love song to her when they had first met. She would touch his empty pillow when the song was done and wish him goodnight.

The washing up was finished and she glanced at the whey-faced clock above the kitchen window, a pale imitation of its celestial counterpart.

"Dead on ten," she noted.

Routine had become almost as important to Mrs Murgatroyd, as her songs. It would have been so easy to drift through her days, without purpose or meaning. Each day, she rose at six and each evening, retired at ten. The time between the two points was filled with activities, which were either related to her house or garden, and once a week, she would walk to the shops at the edge of town. Further than that, and it all became too confusing. She found the noise of the traffic threatening, and the people in such a hurry that they would push past her with a disapproving look. Tonight she would be late to bed as, bewitched by the moon, she had been reluctant to leave it. Taking a deep breath, she filled her lungs and sang its praises again.

*"We're very wide awake, the Moon and I"*

As she reached the end of the verse, she was startled by a small sound from somewhere close by. She stood in silence for a minute and listened, but the only sound she could hear was the dripping of the tap. Once again, she sang the chorus, and there it was once again: a small sound, almost an echo of the last word. She peered into the garden, but could see nothing. Cautiously, she slid the bolt on the kitchen door and turned the key. Her daughter always warned her to keep the door securely locked at night, so she opened it just wide enough to be able to peer out into the darkness. A wave of ice cold air met her, making her cheeks tingle and her eyes water. Seeing nothing, she called out, "Hello, is there anybody there?"

Receiving no reply, she told herself that she was imagining things and quickly locked and bolted the door again.

"Moonstruck," she muttered to herself, "that's what you are, moonstruck!"

As she turned to make her way across the room, she froze, for there in the middle of the kitchen, in a pool of moonlight, sat a cat. Its fur, a snow-white puff ball, glistened, while its bright blue eyes flashed like sparks to rival the stars above.

She would laugh the next morning when she would recall saying, 'Where have you come from?', as if anticipating an answer, but now she found the way the cat fixed her with its unwavering gaze, disturbing. She hurried across the room and switched on the light, while the cat continued to watch her closely. The warmth of the kitchen was causing the ice crystals on the tips of its whiskers to fall gracefully to the floor, and its fur to lie wet and flat against its body, as the frost turned to water.

"Poor thing," she said, "you'll catch your death!"

Taking an old towel, she knelt beside the cat and gently patted it dry, working away until its coat resembled a pure, white pom pom. She smiled as her efforts were rewarded with loud purrs and the cat nudged her hand affectionately. Spontaneously, she began to sing a song that her children had loved,

"... *the cat came back the very next day,*
*The cat came back, we thought he was a goner,*
*The cat came back, he just wouldn't stay away"*

As she reached the end of each line, the cat chirped a response, and an inexplicable feeling of happiness rose inside Mrs Murgatroyd, one that she had not experienced for many years.
"You're a clever one," she said with delight, then suddenly, her mood changed and she added, "Someone must be missing you. Someone must be worried."
Reluctantly, she opened the kitchen door and called to the cat, "Come on, out you go!" She clapped her hands to encourage it to move, but it remained in the centre of the kitchen floor. It deployed that cat's trick of ignoring what did not suit it, and started to groom itself with long, slow licks of its tongue.
"Well, I suppose one night won't matter ..."
Having provided her visitor with a few scraps of cold chicken, a saucer of water and an empty box in which to sleep, she closed the kitchen door and went to bed. It was not until her head hit the pillow, that she realised that *The Grand Old Duke of York*, *Brahms Lullaby* and *Beautiful Dreamer* had all been forgotten, but before closing her eyes, she kissed her finger tips and placed them on the empty pillow and whispered, "Goodnight". Her

eyes had started to close when the soft padding across the bed, a moment of kneading and a softly purred lullaby announced the cat's arrival.

When she woke at six the next morning, the space where the cat had lain was empty.

"Moonstruck!" she scolded herself, thinking that her visitor had been nothing more than a figment of her imagination, but when she entered the kitchen a few minutes later, the cat was sitting near to the kitchen door.

"Oh, well," she said sadly opening the door, "nothing lasts forever."

However, after a few minutes in the garden, a faint mewing signalled the cat's return.

"What am I going to do with you?" she pondered as she watched the cat eating the last of the chicken. At that moment, she heard her neighbour's door slam, and quickly went to her front door and opened it. She searched her memory for the young woman's name and remembered it just before she had reached the garden gate.

"Emily!" she cried.

Her neighbour stopped and turned, surprised by this sudden contact with a neighbour, who usually kept herself to herself.

"Emily," Mrs Murgatroyd repeated, "I'm sorry to bother you, but do you know if anyone has lost a cat? It's white and obviously very well cared for."

It was only when the girl turned and she read the logo on her jacket, that Mrs Murgatroyd remembered that Emily worked at the animal rescue centre in the town. Her neighbour's glance towards the end of the road told Mrs Murgatroyd that she was in a hurry, probably catching a bus, or being given a lift to work.

"I'm sorry, you'll be late  ..." she started to say, but to her surprise, Emily closed her gate and walked up Mrs Murgatroyd's path.

"Many cats are chipped, these days," she said, and being met with a blank stare, explained how microchipping worked. While Mrs Murgatroyd stood by like an anxious parent, Emily examined the cat and offered to take it to the centre.

"We can scan for a chip," she said. "If there is one, it will tell us who the owner is."

"Could I ...," Mrs Murgatroyd hesitated.

"Come with her?" Emily finished the sentence. "Of course. Let me just make a phone call."

A few minutes later, a van pulled up and a young man  carrying a cat carrier made his way up the garden path.

In less than half an hour, the cat and Mrs Murgatroyd had been driven to the centre, the scan carried out and they now sat in the reception area, anxiously waiting while the database was searched. Her eyes stayed fixed on the office door, a sense of foreboding growing by the minute. Finally, the door opened and the young man who had collected them appeared.

"Good news!" he started, then realising that what he had to say would not be welcome, continued less enthusiastically.

"The cat is registered to a lady in the next street to yours.  We'll take her round now." In an attempt to soften the blow, he added, "Her owner will be most grateful to you. Would you like to come along, then I can drop you home."

Mrs Murgatroyd nodded her thanks and a few minutes later, found herself outside a house, not dissimilar to her own. The young man's knock on the door was answered by a woman, whose red-rimmed eyes served as a testament to her grief. She had obviously been worried by the cat's disappearance and Mrs Murgatroyd felt ashamed that her selfishness had caused so much distress.

"Mrs Eveline?" the young man asked.

"Miss," came the reply. "My mother was Mrs Eveline."

The young man explained that her cat had been found and was being returned. This news was not met with gratitude, in fact it seemed to have the opposite effect, and succeeded in setting off a fresh wave of weeping.

Between sobs, Miss Eveline informed them that her mother had died, quite recently and quite suddenly.

" … And the cat is just another problem to be sorted out!" she whimpered. She explained that she had a dog and would not be able to take on the cat. She turned to Mrs Murgatroyd.

"I don't suppose …"

"I could take her?" Mrs Murgatroyd could hardly contain her excitement.

"Luna is a good cat. She won't be any trouble."

"Her name is Luna?" asked Mrs Murgatroyd.

"Yes, my mother named her after the goddess of the moon. I wondered what had happened to her. She was never a cat to wander off. Our neighbour thought he saw her disappearing round the corner as he passed the door last night. My mother was putting the empty milk bottle on the step and he wished her goodnight. As she stood up, he saw her clutch her chest and fall to the ground. The doctor said it was a massive heart attack, and nothing could have been done." She dabbed her eyes and took a deep breath.

"What time was this?" asked Mrs Murgatroyd.

"He remembered the time on his phone as he dialled 999. It was dead on ten."

"Dead on ten," Mrs Murgatroyd mumbled, and felt a slight breeze ruffle her silvery hair.

It was soon agreed that Mrs Murgatroyd would adopt Luna, and after collecting her basket and a few pouches of cat food, soon found herself back in her cosy kitchen.

"Keep her in for a few days," the young man advised. "She'll be less inclined to wander." He had reached the door when he turned and added, "Oh, and by the way, Merry Christmas!"

In all the excitement, she had forgotten that today was Christmas Eve and tomorrow was Christmas Day. She returned his greeting and had just sat down in her kitchen, when another knock came at the door. On opening it, she was surprised to see her neighbour, Emily, standing on the doorstep, her arms laden with gifts.

"Everyone at the Centre wanted you to have these," she said. "We receive so many donations of toys, blankets and so on, that we don't know what to do with them all, and after your kindness in taking in Luna, we thought you might find a use for them."

Mrs Murgatroyd thanked her, but it was apparent from Emily's reluctance to leave that there was something else.

"It's about tomorrow," she started tentatively. "We wondered if you would like to join us for Christmas dinner. It's just family and a few friends. Nothing special." She caught the old lady's half glance towards the back of the house and quickly added, "Of course, we realise that you won't want to leave Luna so soon, so we thought you might like to bring her too!"

The next morning, Mrs Murgatroyd put on her best dress and the pair of earrings that had been her husband's last gift to her, and after tying a red ribbon to Luna's collar, carefully carried the cat to Emily's door.

"I know red is not your colour," she whispered to the cat, "but it is Christmas and one must make an effort."

The warmth of the welcome she received brought back memories of the days when her own children had lived at home. When the meal was finished, the guests, full and content, sat in front of the blazing fire while Emily served coffee. As she passed a cup to Mrs Murgatroyd, she was pleased to note that her guest was at ease, humming quietly to herself, her cat on her lap.

"I love to hear you singing," she said. "It always cheers me up!"

"Oh, dear," said Mrs Murgatroyd, "I hope I don't disturb you. I can't help it, you see. The songs just pop into my head and have to make their way out."

"In a terrace, it's hard to keep secrets," Emily smiled, "but don't worry, yours is safe with me … as long as you lead us in a few carols."

Realising that it would be futile to protest, Mrs Murgatroyd cleared her throat and began with one of her favourites,

"*Oh Little Town of Bethlehem*," she began.

"Meow," Luna echoed.

"*How still we see thee lie.*"

"Meow."

The audience was captivated and as soon as one song finished, they begged for another duet. Mrs Murgatroyd could not remember a time when she had been happier. As darkness fell, Emily walked her home and thanked her for making Christmas such a memorable one.

In bed that night, she told her husband all about her day, before kissing her fingertips and laying them on the pillow. She felt content, with Luna to her left and her memories to her right. She knew that she was entering a new phase of her life, when some new routines would be merged with old ones.

"Dead on ten," she would say every night, as she carried her supper dishes into the kitchen ... after first checking that Luna was curled up in her basket, of course.'

*My Name* As I carried out research for a short story about reincarnation and the gods of Ancient Egypt, I reflected that the human relationship with cats has changed across the centuries. They were revered as gods by the Egyptians, reviled in the middle ages and have now regained their preeminent position as the rulers of our homes.

My short story, *Time after Time*, deals with the legend of Bast or Bastet, a goddess worshipped in Lower Egypt. She is usually depicted with the head of a cat, and was associated with fertility and protection against disease.

My story is about reincarnation, as Bast, in the guise of Dorothea, an Egyptian Mau, waits to be worshipped once again:

## Time after Time

"It's time," said Dorothea.

I had been waiting for her to speak, since I had returned to the house. The day had started so well: a trip to the butcher's, followed by the greengrocer's and finally, the steady walk up the hill towards home. As I drew level with Number 39, Mrs Johnstone appeared from behind the garden wall. I reflected later, that her ambush must have been planned, as we usually took great pains to avoid each another. I never understood how we had developed such a mutual dislike for one another, but we had done so since I had first moved into the village almost fifteen years before. I think she felt some resentment that someone, whom she regarded as a person of little consequence, owned the best house in the village. She, on the other hand, led an unhappy existence, married to a man who drank excessively.

Her bitterness seems to have grown at the same pace as his drinking, and I was never quite sure which one had given rise to the other. If her thinly veiled jealousy was hard to tolerate, it was nothing compared with the terrier-like instinct with which she pursued something that you would have preferred to have kept hidden.

Usually, we were both content with a perfunctory greeting; a simple nod, or a mumbled, 'Good morning'. However, I was trying to dismiss the feeling that she had been lying in wait, when a sudden rustling in the rhododendrons set off, what would prove to be, an unstoppable chain of events. The tip of Dorothea's tail could be seen disappearing into the undergrowth, as she made her way through those well-trodden secret pathways, known only to a cat.

"Isn't she remarkable?" Mrs Johnstone began. At first it almost seemed to be a compliment, and so, succeeded in catching me off guard. "She never seems to age. How old is she now?"

The digging had begun, and I fumbled for an answer, "Oh, I'm not sure. She came to me as a sort of rescue."

The terrier had taken hold and was shaking me for an answer. "A rescue? I can't believe that so fine a cat could ever be unwanted. Pedigree isn't she?"

I wasn't going to fall into that trap. If she was a rescue cat, I would probably not know her provenance. I swallowed hard, trying to appear as calm as possible. "Her previous owner died and I was asked to take her in." It was a half-truth, after all.

"An Egyptian Mau, isn't she? I looked her up on the internet." She had obviously been doing some research, and that worried me. "Such a fine animal. I wonder that you let her roam so freely. She would fetch a good price in some quarters."

I wanted to snap back that the last man who had tried to steal her was still in hospital, having been found gibbering incoherently about fiends and demons. Instead, I held my tongue, smiled and nodded.

"There's a new Tom at Number 23 and I think he is, you know, intact." She whispered the last word, as if drawing me into a conspiracy.

Again I smiled and tried to reply casually, " Oh he came calling last week and Dorothea soon saw him off!" My amusement was genuine as I remembered the encounter. He had crept up behind her, his mouth open to catch her scent, but when he was within a few feet of her, she had turned and flashed her green-glass eyes with such ferocity that he had bowed his head and retreated in reverse, like an old fashioned courtier paying homage to a great queen.

The church clock struck midday and saved me from further inquisition, as I was able to use it as an excuse to leave. "Oh, is that the time? I must get home. Almost lunchtime!" I quickly took my leave, hoping that my false cheerfulness was not too obvious.

Dorothea was sitting at the table when I entered the kitchen, and watched in silence as I unpacked the shopping. In fact, she took her time, waiting until we had finished our lunch before she said it.

"It's time"

In the words of Terry Pratchett, 'In ancient times cats were worshipped as gods; they have not forgotten this.'

My accidental meeting with *Alice the Book Store Cat* came about when a photograph of her popped up on Twitter. I follow @Readingwithcats and enjoy the beautiful images which they regularly post. Little Alice, a cat long gone, lay on a green velvet chair in the Dusty Bookshelf in Lawrence, Kansas. Research provided information about the cat and her home: The shop aims to 'buy, sell, and trade high-quality, gently read books' and is an Aladdin's cave of literature. Alice's life there is described on the shop's website: 'Alice came to us as a stray in 1999, and she decided she wanted to stay. This sweet girl could always be found on her green chair in the animals and pets section. Sadly, Alice passed away in early April 2014.'

I contacted the Dusty Bookshelf and asked permission to use their photograph and received a heartwarming reply, which said, 'We loved Alice so much and are thankful for any reminder of her... Please feel free to share your wonderful poem with any accompanying Alice photos.'

As T.S.Eliot said, 'Books. Cats. Life is good.'

*The Cat in the Window* : Before the dawn of television, Christmas Eve was traditionally the time for family entertainment of a different kind. As previously stated, everyone would gather around the fireside for games and ghost stories. Many of the stories would be passed off as, 'authentic anecdotes about spectres,' Jerome K. Jerome wrote in *Told After Supper*, an anthology of Christmas ghost stories. In my poem, I have tried to convey an important message for this time of the year, echoing the words of Francis of Assisi:

*'If you have men who will exclude any of God's creatures from the shelter of compassion and pity, you will have men who will deal likewise with their fellow men.'*

*The Cat in the Window* was written to perform at a Christmas festival. It was inspired by all of the animal charities, and the sad cases of neglect and abuse they often have to deal with. As the day approached, I realised that I would be unable to read the poem without becoming upset, so chose to read *All Hallows' Eve* instead, changing the title to Christmas Eve. I printed small copies of **The Cat in the Window** and left them on chairs and tables around the room.  At the end of the festival, one lady approached me in tears and thanked me for sharing the poem. She later contacted me to say that she had adopted a senior cat from *Cats Protection*.

*The Rescuer*: @HuskattaPusur's Twitter account was one the first I came across - accidentally, of course. His profile states, 'I'm the king of The Norwegian Arctic Cats. My forefathers were the fearless arctic cats whom the Vikings depended on for surviving & conquer distant territories!' Well, he certainly conquered many hearts, because when he died, the largest newspaper in northern Norway wrote, 'The King Pusur is dead'. Hans Halden of Forente Poter (United Paws) has carried on his work with cats in the extreme conditions of the frozen North. I wrote *The Rescuer* for him. At *Pusar's Arctic Kingdom*, he is ably assisted by a new team of cats, including King Minos and Queen NeNe.

*Cat on a Greek Island* drew inspiration from the many cats I have encountered on several Mediterranean islands. On Kos, near the great Plane known as the Tree of Hippocrates, volunteers feed the local clowder of feral cats. Kos is a small island, but has an estimated cat population of over thirty-five thousand. Rescue organisations have adopted a *Trap, Neuter and Return* programme in an attempt to control the numbers. On the small, volcanic island of Nisyros, mother cats can be seen shepherding their tiny kittens across the road, training them to avoid the buzzing Vespa scooters in the narrow lanes. A few could be seen sleeping before the beautiful white walls of the Church of the Virgin Mary in the Main Square, Nikia. But it is on Cyprus where cats are most revered. One breed is even named after the island, being known as the Cyprus Cat, Saint Helena or Saint Nicholas cat. Local legend tells that Saint Helena arrived in Cyprus to find the monastery in disarray. A drought had caused snakes to invade the building, as they searched for a water supply. Many of the monks were afraid to stay and had left the island. She decided to have a thousand cats sent by boat to Cyprus from Palestine and Egypt.

The monks took care of the cats by feeding them twice a day and providing shelter at night. A bell summoned the cats to supper, and when they had eaten, the cats of Cyprus dealt with the snakes.

*After Passchendaele*:  It is said that unless you are  extremely famous, no one will remember you one hundred years after your death. Each year, I buy a new poppy from the Royal British Legion Poppy Shop,  in readiness for Remembrance Day in November. I have quite a collection now, ranging from bright, little, enamelled lapel pins to bejewelled brooches set with Siam red and olivine green stones. However in 2017, I bought a small, simple pin which was commissioned to commemorate the one-hundredth anniversary of the Battle of Passchendaele, also known as the Third Battle of Ypres. My grandfather's regiment was engaged in the conflict, and although he was invalided out soon after, at least he survived.

It was one of the largest battles of World War I, resulting in devastating losses on both sides.  In this one battle alone, 60,083 British soldiers died in fields that had been turned to a quagmire of mud by torrential rain. What lies beneath this figure is the fact that many of those who died were young men who had not even reached voting age, which was twenty-one at the time. That fact was brought home to me when I unpacked my poppy and found a commemorative certificate alongside it. It gave details of a British soldier whose life was lost one hundred years ago during the 103 days of the Battle of Passchendaele. I decided to find out more about 'Private Tarr', and easily found him on the Commonwealth War Graves Commission website. I knew his service number, his rank and regiment and the location of his memorial, but what my certificate had not told me, was that he was only nineteen at the time of his death. My sense of loss for this soldier was palpable: I thought of all of the experiences I have enjoyed in the years since my nineteenth birthday and how they had been denied to him. He never married, had children or grandchildren, or returned to this peaceful country of ours which, despite its flaws, is still a beautiful place to live. When someone asked me what the poppy cost, my reply was that it was 'priceless'. Perhaps it would have been more accurate to have said that it was, 'beyond price'.

On 4th October each year, I wear my little pin with pride and remember Private Frederick Tarr, even though he was not famous and it will be more than one hundred years since his death.

His sacrifice triggered another memory. As a student returning to my lodgings, one night more than fifty years ago, I heard loud cries coming from a house as I passed. A neighbour explained that the man had been shell-shocked during the war. As it was 1968, I assumed that it must have happened during World War Two, but in fact, he had fought at Passchendaele in 1917. The memories of that place had remained with him for more than fifty years, and the memory of his suffering has remained with me for fifty more.

*Cat o'Clock* will chime with anyone who shares their home with a cat. Given that they sleep for between fifteen and twenty hours a day, I often wonder why they decide to be at their most active when I am my least. I once spent three hours between two and five in the morning, trying to catch a mouse that Dotty had lost in the lounge. I never found it, but I suspect that she did.

*Arthur the Aga Cat* was inspired by a photograph sent to me by a friend. It showed Arthur doing what cats do best, sleeping in the warmest place in the house. He was the alpha male of the farmyard, but also loved his creature comforts.

*The Fearless Five*

*Past the Town of Tribulation and Straight on to Derring Do* was my 'accidental book'. It changed the direction of my life and provided a positive focus, at a time when I was facing a personal challenge.

I had just finished a five week course of radiotherapy, following cancer surgery, and had been impressed by the facilities at the Macmillan Renton Unit in Hereford. The unit had received extensive funding from the charity, Macmillan Cancer Support. What happened next determined the path which my writing was to take, and is still taking. I decided to gather together several of my short stories and publish them, donating the royalties to the charity. *Twisted Tales: A Collection by Hilary Orme* is an anthology, compiled in order to raise funds for Macmillan Cancer Support. All royalties for 2016 were donated to the charity. The book is a collection of short stories, each with a sting in its tail. Every one is short enough to enjoy over a cup of coffee or under a night cap. There is something to suit all tastes, from little Gothic horrors to light-hearted sketches. To maximise the income for Macmillan, I needed to keep down costs, so I gathered a few 'volunteers' around me. The first, was my elder daughter, who although an archaeologist by trade, is a very competent graphic designer. The second was my sister, who carried out some of my proofreading. She inadvertently planted the seed of the idea to write a children's book, when she reminded me that our mother would tell me to entertain my boisterous sibling by telling her a story. As soon as one was finished, she would say, 'Tell me another'. Sixty years on, my granddaughter made the same request.

In gratitude for her help, I wrote my first children's book and dedicated it to both of them. I was unprepared for the success of the children's book, which soon spawned a series. In the first book, *Past the Town of Tribulation & Straight on to Derring Do*, we meet the characters for the first time.

Their adventures see them tackling thieves, and undertaking a daring rescue on the treacherous River Severn. Dotty, the Salty Sea Cat, is the constant in the stories. Her only failing is that she is often lured by ham sandwiches. Dotty belongs to Grandma, the owner of the yacht, *Fiona*. Grandma's friend is an old salt called Billy O. The stories are told in the first person, from the viewpoint of nine-year old Megan Waterfield. Although at loggerheads at first, Megan befriends Boat Boy Bob and together they are often the catalysts for adventures in the Old Harbour. Together, these characters make up my *Fearless Five*.

At the centre of each of the stories, Dotty reigns supreme. She is a Bengal cat, possessed of all the independence and sense of adventure, which is so characteristic of the breed. She is based on my own cat, who's father was a Bengal cross. We first meet Dotty when she makes a surprise appearance.

*Past the Town of Tribulation and Straight on to Derring Do*

'A plate of ham sandwiches, dishes of strawberries and cream and a big jug of homemade lemonade were laid in the centre of the rug. There was a sudden rustling in the bushes nearby and out sprang a cat with a coat the colour of cinnamon, peppered all over with large nutmeg spots. As she moved into the sunlight, her fur looked as if it had been sprinkled with golden glitter and she announced her arrival with a cry that was half bark and half chirp.

"Dotty, you fusspot!" said Grandma as the cat rubbed against her, purring like a lawnmower. "Lured by ham sandwiches, I think. I know this is just cupboard love!" "Cupboard love?" I thought. "Better not ask!"

"She's beautiful!" I said and as if attracted by a fresh  admirer, Dotty turned, excitedly swinging her long tail to and fro. With one swish, the jug was thrown into the air and as we ran for cover from the lemonade shower, Dotty retreated into the bushes with a ham sandwich in her mouth.

"Hmmm," said Grandma, "I'm not sure about that.  'Handsome is as handsome does'!"

"Better not ask," I thought.'

Later in the story, she is featured in the local newspaper, after a journalist observes her swimming in the harbour, wearing a life jacket marked with the words 'SMALL DOG':

'Grandma read the article out loud to us. It was headed, 'Salty Sea Cat', and told how this special little cat had her own life jacket and loved to do the 'catty paddle' across the inner basin. There was no mention of any of the attractions of the Old Harbour, except for the little Bengal cat who loved to swim there. Grandma would break in to her reading by saying things like, "Look at my hair in that   photograph. What a fright!" and, "I'm glad he mentioned about the Asian Leopard Cat" and so many more interruptions that I thought we would never get to the end. As she  finished, we all declared it to be the best article we had ever read and felt extremely proud to know such an unusual cat.

"Right madam," she addressed the remark to Dotty. "Showtime!". SMALL DOG was strapped securely around the little cat's body and she was carried over the lock, up the cinder path, through the gate and down the steps to the Fiona.  A cheer went up from the crowd as Grandma lowered her into the water. I set about opening the sail locker, so that the net would be ready as soon as she started to grow tired. It was as if she knew that she had an audience of admirers, because she swam for much longer and ventured closer to the far bank than on the previous occasion. When Grandma finally scooped her out of the water with a flourish that made her look like a ringmaster at the circus, the crowd applauded and cheered.'

The Fearless Five go on to have more adventures in *Red Skye Sunset*, when they help Rat Boat Ryan to uncover the truth about the boat, *The Red Skye*.

They work together to catch a kidnapper, tackle bullies, carry out a daring rescue and  deal with rats ... lots of rats.

In *The Intrepid Trotter Malloy*, they battle storms and go on an exciting treasure hunt.

In the final book of the series, *Pevensey the Pirate King*, the Fearless Five are thrown into the dazzling world of movie making, where they encounter a pink bouncy castle, a menacing shipwreck and a scurvy skullduggan.

*Pevensey the Pirate King*

'The Pirate King lingered in front of the portrait of Dotty and remarked,

"She's a fine beast. A very fine beast indeed!"

At that moment, Grandma appeared with plates of ham sandwiches, sausage rolls and unrecognisable small things on sticks.

"Yes, and she's my fine beast," she said firmly. No one called her cat a 'beast' and got away with it, even if he was a famous Hollywood star.

Deep Rivers had developed the knack of ignoring people, if they challenged or annoyed him. After all, he was famous and this old lady was a nobody. He made no response to Grandma's comment, choosing instead to tell the story of his own cat, *Pevensey*.

"We were on location near to Pevensey Bay," he recalled, joining his fingertips and leaning back on his chair. He tilted his head upwards and seemed to be addressing something on the ceiling.

"Delay after delay after delay," he droned. "First the camera crew got sick, then the weather turned nasty and we had three days of gales. We were delighted when, at the beginning of the second week, the sun shone and we were able to start filming near to the Martello Tower. The first scene involved a sword fight between myself and some actor, whose name escapes me."

He waved his hand as if dismissing the man from his memory,

then flicked it round to seize an imaginary sword, which he brandished in the air.

"Suddenly," he continued, "I heard a faint mewing, and peering over the edge, saw a cat, stranded on the rocks below. With the tide coming in fast, there was no time to lose. I jumped down amongst the boulders, grabbed puss by the scruff of his neck and brought him to dry land without a second to spare. When I looked at him, I realised that it was our fate to be thrown together, as he truly is a cat fit for a Pirate King! Of course, there could be no other name for him but *Pevensey*."

Everyone applauded the tale, except for Grandma, who beckoned to me from the kitchen door, saying that she needed help with the teacups.

While I added milk to each cup, she poured tea from a large metal teapot.

"Well, he likes to toot his own whistle!" said Grandma disapprovingly. I had learnt to question my grandmother when she used strange sayings. I was always glad when I did, as sometimes they were funny, sometimes clever and sometimes downright confusing.

Her bad humour quickly disappeared and she smiled, "Why, it just means that he likes to boast."

"You're quite right about that, missus!" One of the pirate crew had carried the empty plates into the kitchen and had overhead our conversation.

"Pevensey Bay? In a pig's eye!" I did not know the man well enough to ask what he meant, but Grandma, being an expert on strange sayings, told me later that it showed that he did not be-lieve the story, one bit.

"The name's Rufus," he said shaking Grandma's hand. "They call me Red Rufus on account of my features," he added. I was unsure if he meant his hair or his cherry red cheeks.

"Mr Rivers is good at finding animals that fit his needs at the time. Before Pevensey, there was Mr Topham, a tuxedo cat. Rivers was starring in a film called *Rainy Day at the Ritz* and Mr Topham fitted the image, because he looked as if he was wearing a dinner jacket and a bow tie. His latest film is about pirates, so Pevensey's goose isn't cooked …yet!"

I didn't need to ask what that meant.

"As for rescuing him from the sea, well if the *Seabourne Cat Sanctuary* counts, I suppose that's true."

I swallowed hard and asked, "So, what will happen to Pevensey when this film is finished?"

The pirate made no reply, but instead drew his finger across his throat, picked up a tray of tea cups and started to make his way back to the Bar.

Unable to hide my concern, I called after him, "And what happened to Mr Topham?"

He did not answer, but just shrugged his shoulders and turned to go once more. I don't know what made me do it, but a feeling of dread had started to creep over me, so I asked,

"And what's his next film called?"

"Oh," said the pirate, "next month he starts filming *The Lost Jungle*."

My fears were obviously shared by my grandmother, because when he had gone, she whispered, "Keep an eye on Dotty. A VERY close eye!"

*Inspector Paw of the Yard*
*The Indifference of Cats*
*My Favourite Curtains*
*The Office Cat*
*Cat Conundrum*
*Four of my Nine*
*The Music of the Night*


This group of poems is the result of years of observation of my feline companions, and from often being on the wrong end of their paws.

I received some feedback from my website that struck a chord, but not in the way in which it was intended. It described Dotty, the Salty Sea Cat as 'adorable'. Of course, on a good day, she will humour me with a 'High Five,' rub against me, purring solicitously while doing so, and actively seek out my company. However, on the majority of days and nights she acts like the Queen of Sheba, demanding to be 'adored' rather than being adorable. This is borne out by how her need to be in my company, is secondary to her desire to show me that she is vastly superior, and firmly in charge. She makes this point by positioning herself above me while I am working in the office, occupying either the top of the printer, or a high shelf.

When the moon is full and the calls of owls, foxes and small scurrying creatures prove too much to resist, she sets about waking her doorman, or in this case, doorwoman. Her first attempts involve finding which part of my body is most accessible. This will usually be an elbow or a toe that has crept from the sanctuary of the duvet cover. The first assault does not involve claws, only a gentle pat from a soft paw. Having failed, the next attack is more concerted, as she brings out the big guns, or rather the sharp claws. By now, I am usually awake, but attempt to ignore her, in the hope that she will settle down again. As she lands on the bed with the force of a Sumo wrestler felling an opponent, I realise that sleep has ceased to be an option. Finally, the 'Wall of Death' is employed. This involves scampering along the landing, in and out of bedrooms and up and down the stairs, and succeeds in forcing me from my warm bed, as I reluctantly return her to the wild.

In *The Intrepid Trotter Malloy*, when Grandma visits Molly Plant, their exchange says it all:
Molly asks, "Have you brought your wild cat with you?"
Grandma answered as any well-brought up child of the nineteen -fifties would have done,
"Yes, Mrs Plant. She is with me, but I have left her in the car, as not everyone likes cats."
"Bring her in," the old lady smiled, "I could not imagine anyone taking a dislike to your cat. Although I think if I was three feet smaller and she was three feet taller, she would have me for breakfast!' "

*Hollow*

The final poem was inspired by all of the cats who blessed me
with their presence, but are no longer with me.  I have never
'owned' a cat, but have been owned by many. Their loss is real,
as anyone who has experienced the death of a pet will know.  At
various places in my garden, they are buried: one near the pond,
another beneath a damson tree, all in places they loved, when
they hunted in the hedgerows or climbed trees in the orchard.
Their physical presence is no more, but each one has left a
cat-shaped hole in my heart.

## ABOUT THE AUTHOR

Hilary Orme is the author of the *Salty Sea Cat* books. There are four titles in the series: *Past the Town of   Tribulation and Straight on to Derring Do, Red Skye Sunset, The Intrepid Trotter Malloy* and *Pevensey the Pirate King*.

The author has had stories published in national  magazines, such as *Aqui*la.

She has a collection of short stories for adults, entitled *Twisted Tales: A Collection of Short Stories*.

She served as a Headteacher and as an Educational Consultant prior to retirement in 2008. She lives with her family, and of course, Dotty the Salty Sea Cat, in a cottage on the Welsh Border.

She is currently writing *Chariot of the Sun,*  a fictional account of the final days of Oliver Cromwell. This will be published under the name, Hannah More.

Printed in Great Britain
by Amazon